The Baby in the Manger

Text copyright © 1995 by
Random House Value Publishing, Inc.
All rights reserved

This edition is published by Derrydale Books,
distributed by Random House Value Publishing, Inc.
40 Engelhard Avenue
Avenel, New Jersey 07001

Random House
New York • Toronto • London • Sydney • Auckland

Printed and bound in China

A CIP catalog record for this book is available from
the Library of Congress

ISBN 0–517–14741–6

8 7 6 5 4 3 2 1

The Baby in the Manger

Illustrated by
Margaret Evans Price

Written by
Isabel C. Byrum

Derrydale Books
New York • Avenel

In Bethlehem, I've heard them say,
Upon a Christmas morn,
Within a stable rough and rude,
The tiny child was born.

There are many stories I have heard
Of Santa and his sled,
Said Carol opening wide her eyes,
And sitting up in bed.

But, of them all, I really think
    I like the best to hear
About the little child who came
    To bring to all good cheer.

While far away in distant plains,
> Some shepherds tending sheep,

Were wakened by a lovely song,
> When they were fast asleep.

And in the sky, three wise men saw
    A star all clear and bright,
Which led them to the little child,
    By its great brilliant light.

And then they say, that little child
    Was sent by God above,
A special gift, to all the world,
    To show how great His love.

I wonder how the angels felt
    When Jesus left the sky;
And if they, like the wise men, saw
    Him in a manger lie.

And if the angels brought Him gifts
    That were in Heaven prepared;
And if they sparkled like the stars,
    And if the baby cared.

I wonder if the men that night
   Told stories they had read
About the Christ that was to come;
   And what the prophets said.

How glad his Mama must have been
    To have so dear a child;
When these good wise men gave him gifts
    I think she must have smiled.

And felt that her own little son,
    So sweet and so small,
Would someday be a noble man,
    Be handsome, and very tall.

Perhaps she felt both grieved and sad,
    Because her baby's bed
Was nothing but a manger rude,
    Where cattle oft were fed.

And then again, she may have thought
    Of Gabriel's words so grave,
Of how he said her child should be
    A prince, the world to save.

She might have heard an echo, too,
    From that sweet midnight song
Which made her think her son would grow
    To be both brave and strong.

Then when the shepherds came and told
    Of angels in the sky
Who said the baby Christ was born,
    She knew that God was nigh.

Perhaps she saw them clasp their hands,
    And heard them sing the song
That had been sung the night before,
    By that vast heav'nly throng.

"Oh glory, glory be to God,"
    Because that Christmas morn,
The tiny babe, who was the Christ,
    In Bethlehem was born!

These shepherds on the plains were told
    The story from the skies;
And carried it to Bethlehem—
    A glad and sweet surprise.

And wise men in another land
    Were led o'er plains so far,
Right to the little manger bed
    Of Jesus, by a star!

What she then thought I do not know,
    My stories do not say.
But certainly their splendid gifts
    Drove all her grief away.

I think that babies all are sweet,
    But none are quite so fair
As Jesus was in Bethlehem,
    Within the manger there.

I wish that I could see that star,
      That lovely song could hear;
Could hold that baby from above,
      Who was to God so dear.

Could visit Bethlehem, and there
      Right where the child was born,
Just lay for him some gift to see,
      Upon this Christmas morn.

And Carol bent her little head
>To pray a silent prayer
To Christ, who once in Bethlehem,
>A manger had to share.